SEASONS SEASONS SEASONS SEASONS

WINTER

Moira Butterfield

Illustrated by Helen James

W

FRANKLIN WATTS

LONDON•SYDNEY

An Appleseed Editions book

First published in 2005 by Franklin Watts
96 Leonard Street, London EC2A 4XD

Franklin Watts Australia
Level 17/207 Kent Street, Sydney, NSW 2000

© 2005 Appleseed Editions

Designed and illustrated by Helen James
Edited by Mary-Jane Wilkins

ISBN 0 7496 6003 1

A CIP catalogue for this book is available from the British Library

Photographs by Corbis (Craig Lovell, Joe McDonald, Richard Hamilton Smith,
Craig Tuttle, Kennan Ward, Staffan Widstrand, WildCountry, Haruyoshi
Yamaguchi, Michael S. Yamashita)

Printed and bound in Thailand

Contents

All about winter

Winter is a season, a time of year which can bring chilly shivers, long dark nights and crunchy snow.

The sun gives us life. Without it there would be no animals or plants on our planet.

Our year

The sun is a huge fiery ball of burning gas which gives us our warmth and light. Our Earth travels around the sun. It takes one year to go all the way around.

Earth words

The two halves of the world are called the northern and the southern hemispheres. While one has winter, the other has summer. The area around the middle of the world is called the equator.

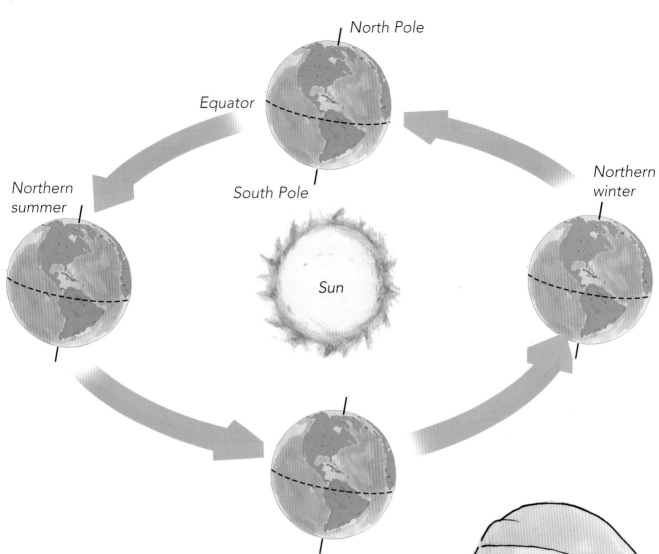

North Pole

Equator

South Pole

Northern summer

Northern winter

Sun

Our seasons

The Earth leans towards the sun as it travels around it. The half nearest to the sun has summer, while the other half has winter. So as the Earth gradually turns around, the seasons change.

Worst winters

The sun's rays are weakest at the far northern and southern parts of our planet, called the poles. The poles have the coldest winters in the world.

5

My winter, your winter

Winter does not come at the same time for everyone. While you shiver in the winter cold, someone on the other side of the world could be sunbathing!

Winter north and south

In the northern half of the Earth winter comes in December, January and February. In the southern half winter comes in June, July and August.

What about the middle?

In countries along the equator it is hot all year round. There is no winter or summer and places have wet and dry seasons instead.

Days and nights

As the Earth travels round the sun it spins in space like a top. It takes 24 hours to spin once. First one side faces the sun, then the other, giving us days and nights. In winter days are shorter and nights are longer.

Around the equator there are wet and dry seasons instead of summer and winter.

Some parts of the world, such as parts of North America and northern Europe, have cold, snowy winters.

Some parts of the world, such as Australia, have rainy, cool winters, rather than lots of snow.

6

Dark all day

The North Pole, at the far north of the world, looks like land, but in fact it is frozen sea. In winter it is dark all day and all night here, and the temperature falls so low that the sea freezes over for many kilometres around.

In Northern Russia people travel on horse-drawn sledges over the February snow.

Colder than a freezer

At the far south of the world there is an area of land called Antarctica. It is so cold there that the land is always covered in ice. In winter it is dark all day and all night. The sea turns to ice around the land and the temperature is colder than a freezer.

Winter's coming

When winter is coming the weather grows colder and the nights last longer. Look out for these winter signs.

Birds leave

A lot of birds leave winter lands for somewhere warmer. You may see them flying overhead in big flocks, on their journey away from the cold. You see fewer animals in winter. Small insects die and other creatures hide away from the cold.

Bare trees

Look down and you will see fewer plants than in summer. As the weather grows colder, plants stop growing.

Look up and you will see deciduous trees (trees that lose their leaves) standing bare of leaves.

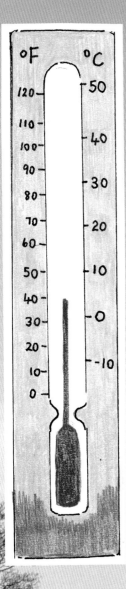

Can you feel winter?

You can feel winter coming because the temperature falls outside. We measure temperature with a thermometer. Coloured liquid inside squeezes up a thin tube as it gets warmer, and falls down the tube as it gets colder. Numbers along the tube measure how far up the liquid gets.

These numbers show the temperature, measured in degrees Celsius (°C) or degrees Fahrenheit (°F).

Winter goosebumps

When skin is cold, little pimples called goosebumps appear. Tiny muscles under your skin tighten, making the hairs on your skin stand on end. Your body wants the hairs to trap warm air around you.

Shivery winter

When you feel cold and start to shiver it's your body's way of trying to warm you up. Your muscles tighten and relax quickly to make more warmth inside you. Then it's time to put on warm winter clothes!

Winter weather

Water freezes when its temperature drops below 0°C (32°F). That's why some parts of the world have winter ice and snow.

All about snow

When water freezes it makes tiny crystals. In a cold winter cloud these crystals form and then bang into each other to create snowflakes. Each snowflake is made up of over 50 separate water crystals stuck together. Snow can be powdery or thick, slushy or dry, depending on how cold the weather is.

Snowflakes are hexagonal, which means they have six sides.

Snow patterns

Snowflakes have a beautiful patterned shape which can be seen under a microscope. Every snowflake has a different pattern. All snowflakes have six sides.

Winter frost

When the weather grows very cold water vapour in the air turns to ice crystals called frost. Frost settles on the ground, plants, windows, and even on spider webs. The ice crystals crunch when you walk over them.

Bad blizzards

Snow falls in winter can make people's lives very difficult. Snowdrifts can block roads and make travel much harder and more dangerous. A really heavy snowstorm is called a blizzard.

Heavy snowfalls can block roads.

Winter garden

In cold winter weather plants stop flowering and growing. They wait for warmer days to return.

Saving water

Plants suck up water from the ground through their roots. In winter this gets harder because the ground freezes. Plants must use less water, so they stop growing and may die down to the ground, ready to shoot up again in spring.

Leaves that lose water

Flat wide leaves (called broad leaves) lose a lot of water. It evaporates out into the air through tiny leaf holes, called pores. To save water, broad-leaved trees lose their leaves in winter. They are called deciduous trees.

Deciduous trees lose their leaves in winter.

Winter buds

In winter a deciduous tree has no leaves but it does have winter buds on its branches. Inside each little bud are new leaves and flowers ready for next year. As soon as the weather gets warmer, the bud will swell and unfold.

Trees have winter buds on their branches.

12

Leaves like needles

Trees that keep their leaves all year are called evergreen.
Their leaves are often shaped like thin needles. These
leaves hardly lose any water through evaporation, so
the trees can safely keep them through the winter.

Shaped for snow

Conifers are evergreen trees that are good at growing in cold, snowy places.
Their branches slope downwards because that makes it easy for snow to slip
off. Otherwise, a heavy winter snowfall could easily break off a branch.

13

On a winter farm

In the winter cold the farmer's fields seem quiet and empty, but there are still plenty of farm jobs to do.

Changing the soil

It might look as though nothing is going on in the fields, but something does happen to the soil in winter. When it freezes and thaws, the top layer breaks into smaller pieces. That makes it easier to plant in spring.

Feeding the animals

There is not enough fresh grass for farm animals to eat in cold winter places. Instead farmers feed them hay made from grass cut on the farm earlier in the year. The hay is stored in bundles called bales.

Feeding people

In snowy places there are no fresh crops for people to eat. In the past people ate food they had stored earlier in the year, such as grain made into bread and fruit made into jam. Nowadays many people simply eat food flown in from other warmer parts of the world.

14

Staying inside

In a harsh winter the weather is too cold for cattle to stay outside. Instead they are kept inside a cowshed. Every day the farmer makes sure they are well fed and that their living areas are kept clean.

Woolly and tough

Sheep can stay outside because their woolly coats keep them warm. They eat hay put out by the farmer. In the mountains of Peru in South America, farmers keep alpacas. They have shaggy coats that are good for making wool.

Alpacas in the snowy Andes mountains. They stay warm because of their thick shaggy coats.

Winter wild animals

In a cold winter it's hard for wild animals and birds to survive. There isn't much food around, and it's difficult to keep warm.

Finding winter food

Hunter animals search for winter food, but it's hard because many of the creatures they eat in summer disappear in winter. Creatures such as foxes go into towns to look for food among human rubbish.

Saving winter food

Some creatures gather a food store to eat during winter. Squirrels and mice hoard food such as nuts and acorns which they gather in the autumn. These little animals huddle together in their dens to keep themselves warm.

European foxes go to towns to search for food in winter.

Winter fur

In snowy, cold places furry animals often grow thicker fur to keep them warm through the winter months. Some animals, such as snowshoe rabbits and weasels, change the colour of their fur to blend in with the snowy background.

Goodnight!

Some animals, such as bears and bats, hibernate in winter. Bats gather in caves where it is cool and damp. Sometimes they return to the same perch year after year.

Bears look for a warm, dry place to sleep in winter.

The toughest ones

Imagine surviving a freezing winter in the Arctic or Antarctic. Some animals brave the snowstorms and some leave for a warmer winter home.

See you in spring

Many polar creatures migrate, travelling away from winter storms to somewhere warmer. Caribou (also called reindeer) travel south from the Arctic in huge herds of more than 100,000 animals.

I'm staying

Many birds leave the northern Arctic in winter, but a few stay and put up with the cold. The brilliant white snowy owl stays to catch any small rodents that venture out, and eat any dead animals it spots in the snow.

Shaggy musk oxen

Musk oxen stay put in tough winter Arctic conditions. They have long shaggy coats to keep them warm. They look for mosses to eat in patches where the wind has blown the snow away.

Polar bear hunters

Lone male polar bears roam the frozen winter sea ice of the far north, hoping to catch a seal when it comes up to breathe through a hole in the ice. Female polar bears hide in a den dug in a snowdrift. They give birth to twins during the winter.

Cosy underground

Small rodents called lemmings scuttle around in underground burrows underneath the Arctic snow. They eat underground plant shoots to keep themselves alive.

Tough insects

In Antarctica it can be −59°C (−75°F) in July. Only a few creatures can survive. Tiny insects called mites and springtails stay alive trapped in the ice. They have a substance called antifreeze in their blood that stops them freezing solid.

Winter stories

All over the world there are legends about the seasons. Here are some winter stories.

An Iroquois Native American legend

The mighty god of all the winds was called Gaoh. He lived up in the sky. He summoned the Earth's creatures to help him with his work, and a giant bear called Yaogah answered his call. "You shall be the freezing north wind," Gaoh commanded the bear, and he tethered Yaogah outside the north door of his home.

When the north wind blows the Iroquois say that the bear is prowling in the sky. They say that Gaoh has unleashed Yaogah, and the bear's icy breath makes the world freeze.

An Inuit legend of the far north

This tale explains why the sea of the far north is icy. One day a famous Inuit hero called Kivioq was in his kayak when a storm blew him to a land he had never seen before. This was the home of an evil sorceress, who tricked humans into staying at her house, and then killed them.

A friendly spirit warned Kivioq and he escaped just in time, rowing out to sea in his kayak. The sorceress was so angry she turned the water to ice, but Kivioq still managed to escape.

All about Jack Frost

Have you heard of Jack Frost?
He comes from Scandinavian
legend. He is said to be a
magical elf who makes the
beautiful frost patterns on
leaves and windows. He is
usually drawn to look as
though he is made of ice.

Winter parties

The longest night of the year is called the solstice.
In the northern hemisphere it is on 21 December.
In the south it is on 21 June.

Christmas lights

At Christmas the birth of Christ is celebrated in many different ways in Christian countries around the world. Lots of Christmas traditions are linked to ancient midwinter ceremonies. In Sweden Christmas celebrations start on 13 December, when girls wear a headdress topped with candles and boys dress as star boys, carrying star wands. The stars and the candles represent the coming of the sun and the melting of the winter snows.

New Year

New Year is celebrated in different winter months around the world. The Tibetan people celebrate their New Year, called Losar, in February. They hold a parade with 1001 twinkling lanterns and candles. In New Zealand the Maori people traditionally celebrate their New Year, called Matariki, in June. They sing songs, dance and clean their homes to signal a new beginning.

Winter fires

Traditional winter parties often include bonfires. The people of the Shetland Islands off the northern coast of Scotland have a big bonfire party on 26 January, called Up Helly Aa. Hundreds of years ago the Vikings who lived on the islands started the Up Helly Aa bonfire ceremony because they thought the fire would help to scare away the long, cold nights of winter.

Snow fun

In February two million people visit the Japanese city of Sapporo for the Yuki Matsuri snow festival. They come to see teams from all over the world carve amazing snow and ice models of animals, buildings, trees and figures. There are even slides made of snow for children to play on.

Paint the winter

Here are some ideas for making winter pictures.

Chilly colours

Blue, white and grey are good colours for winter pictures. They are called cold colours and they remind people of icy winter days.

When you paint shadows on snow, use pale blue. It looks much more realistic than grey or black!

Light on dark

Try using dark-coloured background paper for winter night pictures. Light colours look extra bright on top of a dark background, so it's a good way to show shiny lights like the ones on this Christmas tree.

Making snow

Here are two ways to add falling snow to your pictures. Practise on some scrap paper before you try them on your finished paintings. Make sure the paintings are completely dry before you put the snow on top of them.

Crisp bag snow

Crisp bag snow

Scrunch up a crisp bag. Dab it into white poster paint mixed on an old plate. Then dab it lightly on to a picture to make a snowstorm.

Toothbrush snow

Dip an old toothbrush into white poster paint and hold it with the bristles facing down over the picture. Run your finger along the bristles towards you to make the paint spray out.

Toothbrush snow

Make a piece of winter

Make an edible necklace for hungry winter birds,
and a pretty snowflake to stick on your window.

Birdfood necklace

It is hard for birds to find food in a cold winter when plants and insects
die. Put out food for them, high up where they can eat it safely away
from cats. For this necklace you will need a bag of peanuts in their
shells, a strong needle and some strong thread.

1. Cut a long length of thread. Knot one end
and thread it through the needle.

2. Push the needle through the middle of each
peanut shell, one by one, pulling it down to
the knot at the bottom.

3. When you have enough peanuts,
tie the ends of the thread together
to make a necklace.

4. Hang the necklace on the
branch of a tree or bush, so you
can see it from your window.
Watch the birds come to feed
on your tasty present.

A paper snowflake

Once you have made your first paper snowflake you will want to make lots in different shapes and sizes! Stick them on to your window or make them out of card and fix them on to coloured paper. You will need scissors, a pencil and some coloured paper or card.

1. Draw round something circle-shaped, such as a plate or a cup. Cut round the circle you have drawn.

2. Fold the circle in half. Then fold it into three, as shown.

3. Cut little pieces out of the straight edges, and a little more out of the curved edge.

4. Unfold the paper to see your snowflake. Now make a different one!

27

Be a winter scientist

Discover some winter science by finding out the secrets of ice.

Wildlife watch

Explore the winter wildlife outside your window. All you need is a notebook or paper, some coloured pencils or pens and some bird food. If you can, borrow some binoculars.

Ask an adult if you can put some bird food outside a window. Try breadcrumbs, bacon rind or a bird hanger full of peanuts.

The best time to watch birds is early morning or at dusk, when they come to feed.

Draw each bird you see, and colour it in. Later on, use your drawing to find out the bird's name in a bird book. Label your drawings with the time and date you did them.

Secrets of ice

Ice is frozen water. Experiment with freezing fruit juice, which is mostly water, to find out two ice secrets. You will need two plastic cups, a pen, a fridge and a freezer compartment.

1. Fill the two cups with the same amount of juice (about half full is best). Use the pen to mark the level of the juice on the outside of each cup.

2. Put one cup in the fridge and one in the freezer.

3. Next day, look at your cups. Has all the juice frozen? Look at the juice level in each container. Is it the same as yesterday?

Let the frozen juice warm up a little to soften, and then eat it with a spoon!

Did you get these results?

Water has to be at a temperature of 0°C (32°F) to freeze. Your fridge shouldn't be that cold, but your freezer should be. Water expands (gets bigger) when it freezes, so the frozen juice should be higher up the cup.

Words to remember

Antarctic The frozen land at the far south of the world.

Arctic The frozen sea at the far north of the world.

blizzard A heavy snowstorm.

deciduous tree A tree that loses its leaves in winter.

equator The imaginary line around the middle of the Earth.

evaporate To disappear into the air.

evergreen tree A tree that keeps its leaves all year round.

frost Ice crystals that are made when the weather gets so cold that water vapour in the air freezes and settles on the ground.

hemispheres The two halves of the world – the northern hemisphere and the southern hemisphere.

hibernate To hide away and rest during the winter months. Polar bears hibernate in winter.

migrate To journey from a cold part of the world to a warmer part of the world for the winter, and to make the return journey in spring.

North Pole The furthest north point on Earth. It is on sea which is always frozen.

snowflake A group of ice crystals stuck together to make a six-sided shape.

South Pole The furthest south point on Earth. It is on land which is always frozen.

temperature How hot or cold something is.

thermometer A tube with liquid inside that is used to measure temperature.

winter solstice The shortest day of the year. In the southern hemisphere it is 21 June. In the northern hemisphere it is 21 December.

Index